UNSOLVED **MYSTERIES**

the secret files

Close Encounters with Aliens

Janna Silverstein

the rosen publishing group's
rosen
central

To my mother, Charna Silverstein:
You taught me to open my mind to all the mysteries
the universe has to offer.

Published in 2002 by The Rosen Publishing Group, Inc.
29 East 21st Street, New York, NY 10010

Library of Congress Cataloging-in-Publication Data

Silverstein, Janna.
Close encounters with aliens / by Janna Silverstein.— 1st ed.
p. cm. — (Unsolved mysteries)
Includes bibliographical references and index.
Summary: Traces the many accounts of alien abductions, including both obvious hoaxes and cases that are not easily explained.
ISBN 0-8239-3562-0 (library binding)
1. Human-alien encounters—Juvenile literature. 2. Alien abduction—Juvenile literature.
[1. Alien abduction. 2. Human-alien encounters. 3. Extraterrestrial beings. 4. Unidentified flying objects.] I. Title. II. Unsolved mysteries (Rosen Publishing Group)
BF2050 .S55 2001
001.942—dc21

2001003790

Manufactured in the United States of America

Contents

In 1947, airline pilots E.J. Smith, Kenneth Arnold, and Ralph E. Stevens *(left to right)* study a photograph of the disc they claimed to have seen while flying to Seattle. Is it an aircraft, or is it a UFO?

1
UFOs and Close Encounters

Humanity has always wondered about life on other planets. Books and movies about contact with beings from outer space are compelling because they suggest that we are not alone in the universe. Until the last forty years, however, few fictional accounts have even approached the strangeness of the encounters that people talk about today. Alleged abductees describe lights in the sky, ships that travel at impossible speeds, gray beings with big black eyes, and dim recollections of frightening abductions that haunt them the rest of their lives. What are these people experiencing, and what is the truth behind their stories? And is there some kind of cover-up going on?

It all began on June 24, 1947, a clear, calm day. Kenneth Arnold, a deputy sheriff and businessman, as well as a trained private pilot, was flying his airplane around Mt. Rainier, about ninety miles south of Seattle, Washington. As he flew north, he spotted nine odd objects speeding in a V formation at what he estimated was over a thousand miles per hour. At the time, an unidentified flying object (UFO) was exactly that: an object flying through the air that was unlike any recognizable aircraft. When Arnold described the objects he'd seen as saucer-shaped, the press jumped on the description and dubbed the crafts flying saucers.

Only two weeks after Kenneth Arnold's sighting, rancher Mac Brazel discovered metallic debris spread over acres of his ranch just outside Roswell, New Mexico. Unhappy about the garbage, which he assumed to be military wreckage, he called officials at the 509th Bombardier Group at the local air force base. The military initiated a high-security search and clean-up operation, and followed it with a stunning announcement: the discovery of a crashed flying saucer. Witnesses who examined the debris reported seeing pieces of metal with symbols thought to be writing, and bits of foil that couldn't be burned, creased, or torn.

Several days later, the press release was retracted on orders from General Roger M. Ramey, commander of the Eighth Army Air Force, now in charge of the investigation. Major Jesse A. Marcel, who had been handling the research and recovery mission up to that point, stated that the debris was nothing more than the wreckage of a weather balloon.

The Roswell incident has never been fully explained, despite the testimony of witnesses who saw debris they couldn't identify, firefighters who stated they'd seen a second crash site where alien bodies—

The army air force claimed that this debris, collected from a farmer's field in 1947, came from a weather balloon.

and an alien survivor—were found, and military personnel who admitted to having been part of a cover-up. Was the debris a weather balloon or something much more? Were alien bodies taken away for examination? Was there a survivor? Any physical evidence collected was reportedly shipped out of Roswell to destinations unknown, and to this date, no clear explanation has ever been offered. What's more, many of the Roswell records appear to have been destroyed.

In 1956, the National Investigative Committee on Aerial Phenomena (NICAP) was formed to study UFO encounters in an objective and scientific manner. NICAP investigated reports made by believable witnesses such as pilots, military officers, and scientists. The United States government investigated UFO reports under the code names Project Sign, Project Grudge, and Project Blue Book. These three projects seemed to concentrate on debunking the validity of UFO reports rather than trying to substantiate them. Soon, however, people began to claim that aliens from UFOs had abducted them.

Dr. J. Allen Hynek, who had worked on Projects Sign, Grudge, and Blue Book, founded the Center for UFO Studies (CUFOS) in 1973. Dr. Hynek created the term "close encounters" as a way to classify the kinds of sightings and contact that people reported:

✗   Close encounters of the first kind are UFO sightings within at least 150 yards.

✗   Close encounters of the second kind are characterized by physical evidence such as burn marks on the ground or unidentifiable materials left at the location of a sighting.

✗   Close encounters of the third kind feature UFOs with visible occupants.

✗   Close encounters of the fourth kind are personal encounters with alien entities or abductions.

✗   Close encounters of the fifth kind consist of actual communication between a human and an alien.

Skeptics contend that a civilization advanced enough to travel through space at the speed of light wouldn't bother going all that way to visit Earth, a primitive, backwater planet on the edge of the Milky Way. If this is so, then how do we explain the experiences of people like Betty and Barney Hill, Kathie Davis, Travis Walton, and the thousands of others who tell about their experiences with alien beings? Some stories may be hoaxes or dreams. But we can't explain them all.

2

Contactees, Space Brothers, and the Cosmic Age

The woman standing beside the reporter is brown-haired and well groomed, her bow-shaped mouth carefully lipsticked. In a cultured voice she tells the reporter, "I have made telepathic contact for the past eight years with many space people from many areas of space, both inside and outside this solar system." She is a "contactee," one of the many people who came forward in the 1950s claiming to have been contacted by space people.

In the aftermath of World War II, everything was changing. The press treated both Kenneth Arnold and the Roswell reports seriously; the world was seeing the aftereffects of atom bombs dropped on the Japanese cities of Hiroshima and Nagasaki; and the Cold War between the United States and the Soviet Union was on everybody's mind. It was a time when anything seemed possible.

In 1952, when George W. Van Tassel told the world that he had been in psychic contact with "Lutbunn, senior in command first wave, planet patrol, realms of Schare," it seemed too fantastic to believe, but people listened. As many as 5,000 men and women flocked to the Giant Rock Interplanetary Spacecraft Conventions that Van Tassel founded, held in the California desert. These conventions continued through 1977, and included lectures, panel discussions, book and paraphernalia dealers, and contactees of every stripe telling their tales.

Another prominent contactee was George Adamski, a Polish immigrant to the United States. Adamski claimed, beginning in the late 1940s, to be in regular contact with people from Mars, Venus, and Saturn. He referred to these people as Space Brothers. Described

Giant Rock, a huge boulder rising out of the sand in the California desert, was the scene of George Van Tassel's spacecraft convention in 1952.

as tall, remarkably humanlike, and very good-looking, the Space Brothers had only one message: Humanity should abandon its warlike ways, stop the coming nuclear holocaust, and enter an era of peace and abundance called the Cosmic Age.

Adamski wrote four books on the subject. His second, *Inside the Space Ships* (1959), detailed several meetings with the Space Brothers. Adamski wrote that sometimes he was compelled to drive into Los Angeles and check into a hotel. Once there, he would go to the bar and be greeted by tall, handsome people who would escort him to their small, saucer-shaped scout ship hidden in the

desert. They would then fly off to the mother ship and take him to see the far side of the Moon, where thriving cities shined in the darkness. They showed him pictures of Venus, where metropolitan areas curiously like Los Angeles were located, and

Venus was once claimed by George Adamski to be the home of vast cities.

where people lounged along the shores of crystal clear lakes. As proof of his contacts with the Space Brothers, Adamski presented photographs and home movies of the ships he claimed to encounter and diagrams of the ship interiors.

Expert examination, however, showed the photos and movies to be hoaxes, models suspended on fishing wire. Though Adamski's message of peace is still timely, the weight of evidence against him is overwhelming. With a surface shrouded by clouds that move 300 times faster than hurricane winds and an average surface temperature of 900 degrees Fahrenheit, Venus has no lakes; with no atmosphere or water source, the Moon harbors no sparkling cities on its dark side.

In the 1970s, one more contactee came to prominence. Eduard Meier, a Swiss farmer, told of being contacted telepathically by visitors from the Pleiades, a cluster of stars. These beings traveled in crafts called beamships. They said he was selected to be a "truth officer," to learn what they had to teach and, as Adamski claimed to have been told, to prepare for a difficult life because he would not be believed.

Ultimately, Meier claimed, he developed a relationship with a beautiful blond Pleiadian called Semjase. He kept copious notes of their conversations and presented physical evidence he said was of Pleiadian origin. The most compelling aspect of Meier's story was his remarkable photographs of the beamships. They were crisp, clear images of flying saucers soaring over sunny Swiss mountainsides. There was only one problem: It was all a little too perfect.

Experts were never allowed to look at the original photographs or the negatives. Evidence, such as a metal fragment purported to be part of a beamship, somehow disappeared. Years later, after their divorce, Meier's former wife Kalliope denied that any of the story was true.

It's doubtful that any contactee actually had a close encounter of the fifth kind. Their stories left a legacy that would become a mixed blessing to the history of ufology: a dispute between skeptics made wary by contactee tales, and the open-minded who were astonished at the next generation of alien abduction accounts.

3

The Case of
Betty and Barney Hill

*B*etty Hill's nightmare begins in her car on a deserted road somewhere in the New Hampshire night. There is a roadblock just ahead. A group of uniformed men walks toward the car. Betty and her husband don't know what they want, but they're coming closer and closer.

Suddenly Betty is no longer in the car. The uniformed men escort her into a strange, flat craft. The men lead her husband, Barney, into the craft as well. Betty watches helplessly as he disappears in the opposite direction, down a curved corridor and out of sight. The uniformed men tell her not to worry, that he'll be fine.

They take her to a room and tell her to undress. They give her a physical examination. She doesn't know what they want or why they're examining her. They put a needle in her navel and tell her it won't hurt, but it does and she begs them to stop. When one of them covers her *eyes and tells her she's all right, the pain goes away. They assure her that no harm will come to her, and that when it's all over, she won't remember the incident at all. They won't tell her why they want her, but they promise she'll be allowed to go home.*

On the night of September 19, 1961, the Hills were driving south through the White Mountains in New England. It was a crisp, clear night with a full moon, good for seeing the stars that swept thick and bright over the New Hampshire landscape.

Betty, enjoying the view, suddenly noticed a very bright star. As

the star seemed to get larger, she pointed it out to Barney. They stopped along the side of the road several times to try to figure out what they were seeing. Through their binoculars, Betty and Barney saw a cigar-shaped craft, a sort of

Betty Hill describes to investigators the ship that she and her husband, Barney, holding the diagram, saw in 1961.

airplane without wings, with lights blinking around its edge in green, blue, red, and yellow. No aircraft moves that way, Betty insisted, but Barney wanted to believe it was something he could understand: a small, strangely quiet, airplane. The truth was that Barney was afraid. He didn't know why, but there was something wrong with that light. Stars didn't move that way; satellites moved in only one direction; and regular airplanes couldn't maneuver in such a silent, jerky, mechanical fashion. He kept his fear to himself.

When they stopped again, Barney got out of the car and started walking toward the light. Through the binoculars, he saw a pancake-shaped ship with a double row of windows around its edge. In the windows he saw small figures moving back and forth. One of them was staring right at him. Betty yelled at him to come back to the car. Terrified, he ran, got into the car, and they sped away. Suddenly he and Betty heard an electronic beeping coming from behind. The car shuddered and they felt a strange tingling, a sudden drowsiness, and then . . . nothing.

When the Hills arrived home, it was just after 5:00 AM, two hours later than they had expected. They felt clammy and nervous, unable to remember parts of their drive. They both remembered the beeping sound, and they both remembered realizing that they were suddenly thirty-five miles farther along the road than they'd been a moment ago. What had happened between, however, was a mystery.

Betty reported their sighting to the Air Police at nearby Pease Air Force Base. She wrote letters to UFO experts at NICAP. She cajoled Barney into returning to the places where they'd seen the craft, no matter how uncomfortable they both found doing so to be. Ten days after the sighting, Betty had her strange nightmare five nights in a row, and then never again. There was also still the matter of the missing time. Why had it taken them two extra hours to get home?

Two years passed. Barney developed ulcers and anxiety so acute that it interfered with his work. Finally, the Hills conferred with Dr. Benjamin Simon, a Boston psychiatrist who used hypnotherapy in his practice. In the doctor's office, under hypnosis, the two hours of missing time were revealed.

In chilling detail, Barney recalled a strange group of men stopping the Hills along the road. In particular, he remembered the leader's eyes, crying out, "His eyes were slanted. Oh—his eyes were slanted! . . . I've never seen eyes like that before." Barney described how the men escorted them into the woods to the ship he'd seen in the sky. He and Betty were taken to separate rooms. There, he underwent an intimate and upsetting physical examination. When the exam was finished, he and Betty were returned to the car and sent on their way. Dr. Simon recorded all of Barney's hypnotic sessions and planted a suggestion that Barney wouldn't remember the sessions until he was prompted. Dr. Simon then hypnotized Betty to see what she remembered.

Betty's tale was even more bizarre. Just as she had dreamed, she remembered being taken aboard a craft hidden in the woods by the roadside. She described a physical examination that included the sampling of hair, skin, and fingernails, along with the painful needle being inserted into her navel. She recalled the beings telling her this was a pregnancy test. She told Dr. Simon that following the examination, she talked with one of the beings on the ship, who showed her a book and a star chart. Finally, she said, she and Barney were returned to the car and watched the ship depart.

In the weeks that followed, Dr. Simon worked with the Hills, testing their stories to see if any details changed. He was trying to determine if Betty had planted the abduction idea in Barney's mind, if the story was a hoax, or if it was the result of a psychotic episode. He was never able to prove anything, nor were experts from NICAP or military officials from Pease Air Force Base.

The image of the star map Betty recalled stayed with her and she drew a reproduction. It detailed not only stars important to the visitors, but also what were described as trade routes and regular corridors of travel. On April 13, 1965, *The New York Times* published a star chart as part of an article on a new radio source in space called CTA-102. The similarities between the chart published in the *Times* and the patterns in Betty's star map were striking.

The peculiar pregnancy test was the item that intrigued investigators most at the time. In the early 1960s, there were no invasive pregnancy tests being conducted. It wasn't until years later that laparoscopy—the practice of inserting a long, thin tube fitted with fiber optics into a patient's navel for internal observation and surgical procedures—would be developed and used as a regular technique. How Betty Hill could predict such a development in medical technology remains a mystery even today.

4
Kathie Davis
and the Grays

By the time that Kathie Davis (a pseudonym, or false name) wrote to Budd Hopkins, her life was filled with signs of strangeness. She had scars on her body that she couldn't explain. There were geometrical patterns in the yard behind her home in Copley Woods (a pseudonym) where grass had stopped growing. She had dreams of gray-faced beings, "Grays," coming into her home at all hours of the night. Her sister, Laura, had experienced periods of missing time. Her mother had seen lights move in and out of the backyard.

Budd Hopkins is one of the leading investigators in the field of alien abduction. Davis wrote to Hopkins after reading his book, *Missing Time,* which described his work. To her dismay, Davis realized that her personal experiences matched much of what she read about. But there was one major difference: She wasn't the only

Aliens are often described as having large heads and short, narrow bodies.

person in her family to have the peculiar dreams, the strange marks on the body, and the creeping anxiety. She had one clear experience that offered physical evidence.

In June 1983, Mary, Kathie's mother, saw a strange light moving through the backyard. Later that evening, Kathie and two friends went for a swim in the backyard pool and found themselves feeling nauseated. The next day, the ground in the yard appeared to have been burned; the Davis's dog wouldn't go anywhere near it. Over the course of the next three days, the grass in the burned area died off completely. Kathie and her friends suffered continuing nausea. Kathie lost some hair and suffered a sudden onset of eye irritation. In addition, small, scoop-shaped scars appeared on both her and her mother's knees, but neither knew what had caused them.

Hopkins recognized the classic signs of a possible close encounter: the scoop marks on the body, a free-floating anxiety that had no direct association to a clear memory, periods of missing time, and strange marks on the ground. Before he knew it, his list of people to interview included the entire Davis family and neighbors next door and across the street.

First, Hopkins examined the physical evidence. He had soil samples from the Davis yard tested. The burned soil was chemically identical to the normal soil, but it appeared to have been subjected to extremely high temperatures for a long period of time.

Next, Hopkins investigated Kathie's experiences. Under hypnosis, she recalled encounters and abductions that went as far back as childhood. The common element in all of these experiences were the small, gray people who would meet her and take her elsewhere. She recalls that they had large heads, big black eyes, and small mouths. They seemed to speak to her telepathically. The most significant recollections were of her abductions in the late 1970s and early 1980s.

In late 1977, in the company of two friends, Kathie Davis was in a car when they sighted a UFO. Like Betty and Barney Hill, Kathie recalled finding herself paralyzed and taken somewhere to be subjected to an unpleasant and unnerving physical examination. At the time, Kathie was engaged to be married. Shortly after the incident, to her delight she found herself pregnant. She and her fiancé moved their wedding date so they could be married sooner. Then Kathie recalled that just a few months later, in March of 1978, she had another encounter that changed everything.

Kathie was staying at her sister and brother-in-law's home and was feeling nervous and unwell, which she attributed to her pregnancy, still in its early stages. She started to feel drowsy and then, though she was alone in the house, she felt someone massaging her lower back and her shoulders. The experience at first was comforting, then became frightening as she felt herself, as she later described the feeling, being opened up like a flower. First there was pain, then fear.

In the next days, Kathie discovered she was no longer pregnant. She hadn't experienced any of the usual signs of a miscarriage, but suddenly the baby she had been carrying was gone. Her physician couldn't explain it. To Kathie's thinking, it appeared that the gray beings had taken her baby.

In 1983, Kathie recalled, she had yet another abduction experience. She remembered standing in a room with four Grays. She felt anticipation growing in the room. A door opened, and two more Grays came in with a little girl with wispy white hair and large blue eyes. She had a small pink mouth, a tiny nose, and a larger-than-normal head for a child her size. One of the Grays told Kathie to be proud, that this little girl was part of her, but that the little girl must stay with them. Kathie was certain that this was the child the Grays had taken from her. They promised Kathie that she'd see the little girl again in the future and then sent her on her way.

In the years following his work with Kathie Davis, Budd Hopkins met other women who told similar stories of pregnancies that ended prematurely and of being presented with strangely delicate, big-headed children. Other researchers have heard similar stories told by women completely unfamiliar with Hopkins's work or the Davis story. Perhaps, in a very real sense, we do have Space Brothers and Sisters elsewhere in the universe.

5

Believers and Skeptics

Talk to a believer or an investigator and the message is clear: Something otherworldly is happening on Earth. Dr. David Jacobs is associate professor of history at Temple University in Philadelphia, and the author of *Secret Life: Firsthand Documented Accounts of UFO Abductions* and *The Threat,* both on the subject of alien abduction. Also a veteran investigator, he says, "Even if there is only the smallest percentage of a chance that [the alien abduction phenomenon] is real, we should begin to put energy and funding into studying it because the payoff is so enormous. It demands serious attention."

At the other end of the spectrum is Philip J. Klass, the most well-known UFO skeptic. Klass is a retired senior avionics editor of *Aviation Week & Space Technology* magazine, and one of the founders of the Committee for the Scientific Investigation of Claims of the Paranormal (CSICOP). In an interview with *Skeptic* magazine in 1999, he said, "My sole objective is to either find a credible prosaic explanation for a UFO report, or if that isn't possible, then to rush to my typewriter—now my PC—and write the most important story of my life for *Av Week,* which would be the most significant article we've ever published . . ." He's on record for offering $10,000 to the first person who reports their UFO abduction to the Federal Bureau of Investigation (FBI) and whose report the FBI confirms.

Based on their quotes, it looks as though both Jacobs and Klass are on the same side of the alien abduction debate. However, except for their stated interest in discovering the truth— whatever that may be—they

This photo from the air force's "The Roswell Report," released in 1997, shows the dummies the air force claims to have picked up in the Roswell field in 1947 and moved to its laboratory.

have little in common. In fact, the controversy over the possibility of alien contact and abduction has fostered heated conflict in the press, in books, and at conferences across the United States. To discover the kind of passion the subject can provoke, one need look no farther than the case of Travis Walton, an abductee whose experience is a landmark in the history of abduction investigation.

In November 1975, Walton and his six coworkers were in the mountainous Apache-Sitgreaves National Forest of northeastern Arizona. As loggers, their job was to thin a section of the forest to allow for faster growth. At the end of the day, as they slowly drove their pickup truck down the winding mountain road, they noticed a bright light in the woods. At first they thought this was the light from a crashed airplane, but as they drove closer they realized that what they were seeing was no ordinary aircraft. It was a golden, glowing saucer hovering ninety feet off the ground.

Walton, the daredevil of the group, got out of the truck and approached the saucer to get a better look. His friends urged him to come back, but he refused to listen. As he got closer, Walton noticed a quiet mechanical whine. Suddenly, the whine grew into an overwhelming roar. The saucer began to wobble. Walton started

Friends of Travis Walton say he was lifted off the ground by a light beam shot from a flying saucer, as this artist's sketch suggests.

back to the truck. A dazzling blue-green beam shot out of the underside of the saucer and hit Walton in the chest, lifting him off the ground and throwing him aside about ten feet. His body landed on the ground and lay still. Mike Rogers, the driver, panicked. He threw the truck into gear and sped away.

Half a mile down the road, Rogers stopped the truck, realizing that he'd left his best friend behind. Although all the men were frightened by what had just happened, they couldn't in good conscience leave Walton stranded and possibly injured. They drove back for him. When they returned to the spot, however, Travis Walton was gone. So was the flying saucer.

The following days were a flurry of activity as the news of Walton's disappearance spread. The local police organized search parties to comb the mountain forests. UFO researchers from a group called Ground Saucer Watch came to take soil samples and readings for radiation, magnetism, and ozone. The police questioned Rogers and the others closely, suspecting murder, kidnapping, or fraud of some kind. Five of the six men passed lie detector tests, clearing them of any crime and confirming their belief that they'd seen a flying saucer. Later testing confirmed the truthfulness of the sixth man as well. Suspicion remained. Five days later, Travis Walton suddenly returned.

Walton returned to consciousness on the side of a mountain road and, in a daze, called family to come get him. He thought he'd been gone only two hours. His five-day beard growth told a different story. Over the next weeks, Walton's family tried to shield him from the press while he recovered. He was befriended by the Aerial Phenomena Research Organization (APRO) and reporters from *The National Enquirer,* who together sponsored much of the treatment Walton underwent in the wake of his return. He had a physical, had blood and urine samples taken, underwent hypnosis, and took a lie detector test, which he failed due to stress. Walton later passed a lie detector test with more than a 90 percent certainty of truthfulness.

Why bring up the Walton case when discussing believers and skeptics? The Walton case is perhaps the best-documented abduction case in the history of ufology. Seven people all say they witnessed the same thing. Trace evidence from the area in question testifies that something unusual happened there; the evidence is consistent with the findings from other UFO sighting locations. One skeptic, an investigator named Jerry Black, after delving as deeply as he could into the case, couldn't punch any holes in the story. The case is unique in almost every way.

In a court of law, the testimony of seven witnesses along with physical evidence and records from experts in several different disciplines would create a compelling case for any lawyer, except when the case is one of alien abduction. Despite all the supporting evidence, the nature of so fantastic and unnerving a subject makes its reality hard to accept. Skeptics are still challenging the story almost thirty years later. They put forward the theory known as Occam's razor, which states that, all things being equal, the simplest explanation tends to be the correct one. Perhaps the Travis Walton case is the exception that proves the rule.

Part of the debate focuses on the reason for such abductions: Why would visitors from another world be interested in human beings? What could be of interest to people advanced enough to master star flight? One might ask the question in another context: Why would humans be interested in dolphins, pandas, or Siberian tigers? Catch-and-release programs have been regular scientific practice in recent decades. Could alien motivation be so different from our own when the abduction scenario suggests such a familiar study method?

Films like *Close Encounters of the Third Kind*, which included this scene of UFOs in flight, grew from the great interest in UFOs during the 1970s.

Another part of the debate focuses on the idea of contamination. So many of us have seen movies like *Close Encounters of the Third Kind* or watched television shows like *The X-Files* that, skeptics say, it's hard to find someone who hasn't been exposed to the idea of abduction or the image of a gray-skinned alien with a big head and large, almond-shaped eyes. Such images, they say, have so permeated our culture that even people who honestly believe they've been abducted can't be considered reliable; they may have dreamed their experiences and unconsciously incorporated popular imagery into their memories. Investigators say that may be so, but many investigators, like Budd Hopkins and David Jacobs, always withhold certain details from their publicized cases and keep them confidential. These details, they say, are consistent from case to case and can help them recognize a genuine abduction experience.

Budd Hopkins, who investigated the Kathie Davis case and thousands of others besides, believes that the abduction phenomenon is real, but he advocates a rational, even skeptical approach. "Be extremely critical of what you read," he says, "and don't believe it all. It's a field where you can get everything from the most serious, the most carefully reasoned investigation down to every single screwball who comes out of the woodwork. Especially in terms of reading: When you read, use every ounce of common sense you can bring to bear on the subject."

Is that an odd approach for a believer? Not at all. The key to any sound investigation will always be exploring every possibility, examining every shred of evidence, and questioning every statement. The simplest explanation may be the correct one, but once the simplest explanations are eliminated, the fantastic suddenly becomes possible.

6

The Past and Future of Alien Encounters

nvestigators are now examining UFO sightings and alien encounters through the eyes of science, history, folklore, and sociology. Why, they wonder, does this phenomenon seem to be so prevalent today yet has never appeared before? Or . . . has it? After all, from generation to generation, stories of encounters with strange, otherworldly crafts and creatures survive. Has this phenomenon, then, always been with us?

The earliest answer might be found in some of our oldest literature. The Bible includes stories like Ezekiel's vision: Ezekiel describes four creatures, each with four faces, coming out of the sky in a flash of light and fire and wind, riding on a wheel within a wheel like, perhaps, something disc-shaped.

And I looked, and, behold, a strong wind came out of the north, a great cloud, with a fire flashing up, so that a brightness was round about it . . . And out of the midst thereof came the likeness of four living creatures. And this was their appearance: they had the likeness of a man. And every one of them had four faces, and every one of them had four wings . . . And they four had the face of a lion on the right side; and they four had the face of an ox on the left side; they four also had the face of an eagle . . . Now as I beheld the living creatures, behold one wheel at the bottom hard by the living creatures . . . The appearance of the wheels and their work was like unto the color of beryl . . . and their work was as it were a wheel within a wheel.

—Ezekiel, chapter 1, verses 4–16

People in the Middle Ages described being visited in the night by incubi (male) and succubi (female), demons which would slip into their victims' rooms with the purpose of sinful seduction. There are many European and Asian folktales of magical beings abducting people, and the Irish tell tales of leprechauns who lure people away with the bait of hidden treasures.

Even as late as the 1890s, with the Industrial Age in full swing and new scientific marvels being invented every year, people still told stories of seeing things in the sky. From Chicago to San Francisco, people claimed to have observed cigar-shaped ships or dirigibles flying with lights shining down to the ground. Such stories were covered in newspapers, and some even suggested that men from the Moon were building airships.

Every society tries to explain mysteries in terms of its own frame of reference. In our space age, the flying saucers move at rocket speed. The stories from the 1890s, before the age of airplanes, describe the ships as dirigibles. In the ancient eras there wouldn't have been thoughts of aliens from other planets. There would, however, have been speculations about creatures from the Otherworld sent by the gods. What may have appeared to a nun in medieval England as an incubus, might today be described as an alien with an interest in creating an alien-human hybrid. Perhaps yesterday's fairies and demons are today's alien visitors in a different guise.

Another theory being proposed today is that alien encounters are nothing more than encounters with our own biology and the geology of the earth. In Canada, researchers are exploring the connection between geological activity, UFO sightings, and reports of alien abduction. When tectonic plates move, rubbing against each other and breaking and changing shape, energy is released (like striking a flint to produce a spark). The theory goes that spots of light described as UFOs are, in fact, energy flashes resulting from plate tectonics. Such released energy might stimulate the brain, specifically the temporal lobe, to produce images and experiences in sleep or unconsciousness that resemble the experiences that abductees describe under hypnosis. Experiments at Laurentian University in Ontario have demonstrated that sensations such as paralysis, the feeling of others in a room, fear and paranoia, and visions of gray, waxy-faced beings can be provoked by stimulating parts of the brain with minor magnetic waves.

Dr. David Jacobs, however, disagrees. "I do think this [alien phenomenon] is extraterrestrial," he says. "They're here for their own agenda. We don't know where they're from and it doesn't matter." He admits, "What we're dealing with is the weakest form of evidence: human memory retrieved through hypnosis by amateurs." He adds, however, "The stories are greatly detailed, and there is a lot of material that has not been released to the general public. People go missing from the physical environment and come back with unusual scars and bruises. It's an area that cannot be dismissed lightly; it cries out for more serious study."

Budd Hopkins feels the same way. "Evidence has only accumulated on one side: that [alien abduction] is happening," he

Governments may not believe in UFOs, but some people will always study the phenomenon.

says. "New evidence would . . . confirm or discredit . . . it—and that hasn't happened. This phenomenon has yet to be explained."

Is there other evidence about which we know nothing? Does the government really have secret files that even the Freedom of Information Act hasn't uncovered? What is the truth about Roswell?

One thing seems certain: Something is happening to thousands of people around the world. Whether they are encountering demons, angels, leprechauns, simple nightmares, or alien visitors, they are experiencing something unique, something that will continue to capture our imagination and attention well into the future.

Glossary

abductee   A person who has been abducted.

abduction   Commonly defined as the kidnapping of a person for illegal reasons. In UFO phenomena, refers specifically to the capture, examination, and return of human beings by alien visitors.

alien   Commonly described as a foreigner, someone from another country. In ufology, describes a visitor from another planet.

APRO   Aerial Phenomena Research Organization, a worldwide organization that investigates UFOs, abductions, and other paranormal incidents.

close encounter of the fifth kind   Actual communication between a human and an alien.

close encounter of the first kind   UFO sighting within at least 150 yards.

close encounter of the fourth kind   Personal encounter with alien entities or abductions.

close encounter of the second kind   UFO sighting that results in a scar or burn mark on the ground, or the deposit or creation of fragments of unidentifiable material.

close encounter of the third kind   UFO sighting that includes visible occupants.

contactee   A person who claims to be in telepathic or personal contact with aliens.

CSICOP   Committee for the Scientific Investigation of Claims of the Paranormal. Founded in 1976, an organization devoted to skeptical investigation of paranormal phenomena.

CUFOS   Center for UFO Studies. Founded in 1973 by Dr. J. Allen Hynek, CUFOS is an international group of scientists, academics, investigators, and volunteers dedicated to the continuing examination and analysis of the UFO phenomenon.

flying saucer   Popular term used to describe an oblong-shaped unidentified flying object.

Grays   Common name for the most-often described abductor; a being between four and five feet tall with a large head, gray skin, small mouth, and large, black, almond-shaped eyes.

hypnosis   A trance-like state induced by a doctor or hypnotist. In the alien abduction arena, a technique used to enhance an abductee's recall of hidden memories.

MUFON   Mutual UFO Network, Inc. Founded in 1969, MUFON is a nonprofit corporation dedicated, through its volunteers, to resolving the scientific mystery of unidentified flying objects and related phenomena.

NICAP   National Investigations Committee on Aerial Phenomena. Founded in 1956, NICAP is an independent organization created to investigate UFO sightings and related phenomena in a scientific way, concentrating on witnesses with expert backgrounds such as pilots, scientists, and the military.

Space Brothers   Tall, graceful humans from other planets inside and outside our solar system, described by George Adamski and other contactees as messengers to humanity.

UFO   Unidentified flying object. Term coined to describe an object that flies through the air but bears no resemblance in shape or behavior to any recognizable form of conventional aircraft. See also flying saucer.

ufology   The study of UFOs and related phenomena.

For More Information

CSICOP: Committee for the Scientific Investigation of Claims of
   the Paranormal
http://www.csicop.org

CUFOS: The J. Allen Hynek Center for UFO Studies
http://www.cufos.org/

Discovery Channel: Space: Aliens
http://www.discovery.com/guides/space/aliens.html

International Center for Abduction Research (ICAR): Dr. David M.
   Jacobs's Web site
http://www.ufoabduction.com

Intruders Foundation: Budd Hopkins's UFO Abduction
   Research Organization
http://www.intrudersfoundation.org

The Klass Files
http://www.csicop.org/klassfiles

Nebula: UFO
http://www.parascope.com/nebula.htm

Nova: Kidnapped by UFOs
http://www.pbs.org/nova/aliens

SETI Institute: Search for Extraterrestrial Intelligence
http://www.seti-inst.edu

Skeptics Society
http://www.skeptic.com/skeptics-society.html

UFOCity.com
http://www.ufocity.com/

UFO Magazine Online
http://www.ufomag.com/

For Further Reading

Adamski, George. *Inside the Space Ships.* New York: Abelard-Schuman, 1955.

Clark, Jerome. *The UFO Encyclopedia: The Phenomenon from the Beginning*. 2nd ed. Detroit: Omnigraphics, 1998.

Clark, Jerome. *Unexplained!* Minneapolis, MN: Visible Ink Press, 1999.

Fuller, John G. *The Interrupted Journey: Two Lost Hours Aboard a Flying Saucer.* New York: Dial Press, 1966.

Hopkins, Budd. *Intruders: The Incredible Visitations at Copley Woods.* New York: Random House, 1997.

Hopkins, Budd. *Missing Time: A Documented Study of UFO Abductions.* New York: R. Marek Press, 1981.

Jacobs, David M. *Secret Life: Firsthand Documented Accounts of UFO Abductions.* New York: Simon & Schuster, 1992.

Jacobs, David M. *The Threat.* New York: Simon & Schuster, 1998.

Kinder, Gary. *Light Years: An Investigation into the Extraterrestrial Experiences of Eduard Meier.* New York: Atlantic Monthly Press, 1987.

Pope, Nick. *The Uninvited: An Exposé of the Alien Abduction Phenomenon.* Woodstock, NY: Overlook Press, 1998.

Randle, Kevin D., and Russ Estes. *Faces of the Visitors: An Illustrated Reference to Alien Contact.* New York: Fireside Press, 1997.

VIDEO

UFOs: Encounters and Abductions. Produced and directed by Scott Paddor, 100 minutes, A&E Home Video, A Greystone Production, 1998.

Index

ABOUT THE AUTHOR

Janna Silverstein is a writer, editor, and teacher who has published nonfiction in print and on the World Wide Web on a variety of subjects, including books, technology, and travel. Her short fiction has appeared in several anthologies as well as *Marion Zimmer Bradley's Fantasy Magazine*. She is the senior editor, fiction and publishing, for WizKids, a Seattle-based game company. She has been watching the skies since her childhood, but, to her disappointment, has never seen a UFO or experienced a close encounter.

ACKNOWLEDGEMENTS

The author wishes to thank the following people for their help and insight: Wolfgang Baur, Amy Guskin, Budd Hopkins, Dr. David M. Jacobs, Rebecca Loudon, Michael Marano, Josepha Sherman, and Michael A. Stackpole.

PHOTO CREDITS

Cover © Antonio M. Rosario/The Image Bank; pp. 4, 7, 16 © Bettmann/Corbis; pp. 11, 27 © AP/Wide World; p. 12 © NASA/TimePix; p. 22 © Peter Gudynas/FPG International; pp. 29, 33 © The Everett Collection; p. 39 © Liaison/Newsmakers/Online/USA.

SERIES DESIGN AND LAYOUT

Geri Giordano